BC Spirits Cocktail Book

Discover British Columbia's Distilling Culture

SHAWN SOOLE

COPYRIGHT

FriesenPress

Suite 300 - 990 Fort St
Victoria, BC, V8V 3K2
Canada

www.friesenpress.com

First Edition — 2021

Editor: Alexie Glover

ISBN
978-1-5255-9848-7 (Hardcover)
978-1-5255-9847-0 (Paperback)
978-1-5255-9849-4 (eBook)

1. COOKING, BEVERAGES, WINE & SPIRITS

Distributed to the trade by The Ingram Book Company

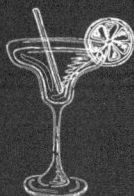

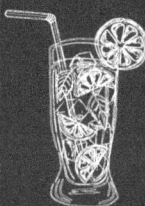

DEDICATION

For the love of all the distilleries in the beautiful province of British Columbia and the people who support them.

INTRODUCTION

Distillation in British Columbia has been around in some form or another for more than 100 years, and not just in the pawned together jerry rigged stills in the bootlegging stories of yesteryear. Huge distilleries existed, supplying both the British Columbia government and our thirsty southern neighbours during Prohibition via the West Coast's "Rum Row."

In recent years, the resurgence of craft distilling in British Columbia has exploded and grown expediently in a way that no other place in Canada has seen in decades. Distilleries in British Columbia come in a variety of forms, such as the minute operations of Sons of Vancouver in North Vancouver and the "bigger" distilleries like Victoria Distillers in Sidney and Okanagan Spirits, which has operating stills in both their Vernon and Kelowna locations.

The provincial government has made moves to make distilling in British Columbia more accessible to the broader market in the province, which has helped spur the industry's growth. Currently, there are more than 75 distilleries in the province, with more in the planning process. These distilleries are as diverse as they are widespread, from Shelter Point on the northern tip of Vancouver Island to True North Distillery in the south Okanagan and everywhere in between. Many breweries have also begun distilling spirits, too, thanks to the abundant supply of barley mash and the easy transfer of the recipes from beer to grain spirit.

There are three main distilling regions in the province: Vancouver Island to the west, Okanagan Valley and the Interior in the east, and Vancouver and the Lower Mainland in the dead centre. Each region has its own subculture of spirits and guest loyalties: those who follow and love craft spirits are fiercely faithful to their cities and area brands. The diversity of the spirits being produced has started to fill the gaps for bartenders to recreate the classic cocktails completely with BC craft spirits, from absinthe to somel or honey rum to amaro and of course, whisky. It's an exciting time for the province and the people dedicated to drinking local products.

VANCOUVER ISLAND

Vancouver Island has always been a hub of craft drinking culture in British Columbia. From the craft beer boom to the growing popularity of wines, Island residents have proven to be loyal supporters of their local craft movements. This consumer curiosity and dedication to locality support, accompanied by bartenders' constant thirst for new ingredients, has led to an explosion of distilleries producing the classic gin and vodka, along with unique specialties such as complex liqueurs and flavourful whiskies.

However you make your way to the island via the multiple ferry ports, airports or heliports, The drive into downtown Victoria is dotted with vineyards, cideries, and distilleries. A 45-minute drive allows you to visit almost a dozen distilleries in the South Island, while a short drive north will open you up to yet another cluster of distilleries showcasing the Island's rural areas. From the Gulf Islands to the west coast of Vancouver Island, you can find almost any spirit you are looking for—all pleasantly paired with amazing scenery and a gorgeous drive.

The island like many regions in the province has it's own microcosm of terroir, the sea air, the snow capped peeks and the warmer summers; this has all pushed the culture of wine, beer and spirits forward on the island with unique adaptions to sourcing ingredients, producers and purveyors. The stories, the region and the terroir is what makes the island a hot bed of drinking culture.

TABLE OF CONTENTS

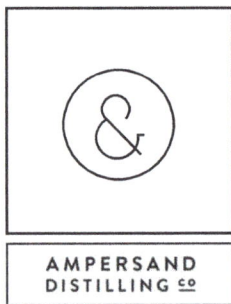

Ampersand Distilling Co.
4077 Lanchaster Road
Duncan, B.C. V9L 6G2
ampersanddistilling.com
250-999-1109

Core Products
Ampersand Gin
Per Se Vodka

Seasonal Products
Nocino!
Imperative Dry
Vermouth
(collaboration with
Rathjen Cellars)

Ampersand Distilling Co. is owned and operated by the Schacht family, whose five-acre organic farm and craft distillery is situated in the heart of the Cowichan Valley. The distillery was created in homage to Jeremy and Jessica Schact's love for craft cocktails.. The business was brought to life when Jeremy and his father Stephen—both trained engineers—combined their knowledge of science and traditional distilling techniques to produce hand-crafted spirits with exceptional flavours. Together, with Jeremy's mother, Ramona Froehle-Schacht (an avid organic farmer), the family fused their individual passions into a thriving business whose high-quality organic spirits have become staples in both industry and home bars across North America.

Ampersand Distilling Co crafts its spirits in a 1000 litre mash tun, 1000 litre pot still, and 500-litre column still, designed and built by Jeremy and Stephen. These custom stills, along with B.C. grown wheat and Ampersand's own spring water, create the companies award-winning Ampersand Gin and Per Se Vodka, as well as its seasonal releases.

Ampersand's name pays homage to the grammatical logogram that forges connections across vast concepts, and the subtle symbol signifies a powerful collaboration between the members of Schacht family. The company brings together science and art, representing the craft of distilling spirits, technology, and tradition. It unites innovative methods and old-world distilling styles, ingredients, and techniques, allowing pure wild-harvested botanicals and B.C. grown wheat to shine, culminating in well-made spirits in which family and friends can share the simple joy of sipping.

BEA ARTHUR

2 oz (60 mL) Imperative Dry Vermouth
½ oz (15 mL) lime juice
½ oz (15 mL) simple syrup
5 fresh basil leaves
soda water

Glass: Collins or highball
Method: Shake all ingredients with ice and strain. Add crushed ice, swizzle, and top with soda water
Garnish: Basil leaves and lime wheel

Created by Cody Dodds

ARBUTUS
DISTILLERY

Arbutus Distillery
1890 Boxwood Road
Nanaimo, B.C. V9S 5Y2
arbutusdistillery.com
250-714-0027

Core Products	Seasonal Products
Baba Yaga Absinthe	Amaro (yearly release)
Blue Gin	Barrel Aged Baba
Canadian Single Malt Whisky	Yaga Absinthe
Citrus Gin	Birch Liqueur
Coven Vodka	Elderflower Liqueur
Crème De Lavande	Forest Dweller Gin
Double Barrel Single	Limoncello
Malt Whisky	Owl's Screech Vodka
The Empiric Gin	Vanilla Liqueur

In summer 2014, Michael Pizzitelli founded Arbutus Distillery in Nanaimo.. Pizzitelli was intent on pursuing his passion for making a plethora of unique spirits and liqueurs under one roof. The distillery aims to infuse a sense of terroir into classic renditions, while also exploring new ones. Much of the distillery's grain from wheat and rye and of course barley comes directly from Vancouver Island. Arbutus also uses local herbs and botanicals, which they grow wherever possible. The distillery also features a lounge and cocktail program designed around its many core and seasonal products—going the entire gambit from raw agricultural ingredients to glass or coupe.

In addition to clear spirits and liqueurs, Arbutus has been producing a variety of whiskies, including single malts and 100 per cent ryes, with other unique barrellings planned for the future.

FOREST DWELLER FIZZ

1 oz (30 mL) Forest Dweller Gin
1 barspoon of Baba Yaga Absinthe
1 oz (30 mL) lemon-verbena syrup
1 oz (30m) lime juice
1 oz (30 mL) egg white

Glass: Large cocktail glass
Method: Dry shake all ingredients, then wet shake with ice, and double strain
Garnish: Rosemary dust

Created by Michael Pizzitelli

7

Bespoke Spirits House
105–425 Stanford Ave East
Parksville, B.C. V9P 2N4
bespokespiritshouse.com
250-228-5385

Core Products	Seasonal Products
Jezabel Gin	Winter Gin
Virtue Vodka	Spring Gin

Bespoke Spirits House is a natural progression in founder and distiller Shelly Heppner's career. Inherently creative, Heppner has always gravitated toward an artistic medium of expression, whether it be designing functional home décor, making her best-selling martini picks, or taking up the art of distilling.

Before founding Bespoke Spirits House, Heppner donned a number of hats in the corporate world, working in retail, telecommunications, insurance, and mortgage brokering. After relocating to Vancouver Island from Vancouver, Shelly visited a farmer's market and was inspired by a local distiller's products. Never one to shy away from a new creative venture, Shelly makes use of her eclectic background and inventive nature to create her signature spirits and unique flavour profiles.

FLORADORA COCKTAIL

1 ½ oz (45 mL) Jezabel Gin
½ oz (15 mL) lime juice
½ oz (15 mL) raspberry liqueur
ginger beer

Glass: Highball or collins
Method: Build ingredients over ice and top with ginger beer
Garnish: Raspberries on a skewer

DEVINE Distillery & Winery
6181B Old West Saanich Road
Saanichton, B.C. V8M 1W8
www.devinevineyards.ca
250-665-6983

Core Products
Ancient Grains
Beekeeper's Honey Shine Silver
Honey Rum
Beekeeper's Honey Shine
Amber Honey Rum
Bianca Vermouth
Black Bear Spiced Honey Rum
Dutch Courage Barrel-
Aged Genever

Genever Dutch Style Gin
Glen Saanich Single
Malt Whisky
Honey Shine Amber
Honey Rum
Moderna Vermouth

Seasonal Products
Sloe Gin
Strawberry Eau de Vie

In 2007, John and Catherine Windsor grew DEVINE from a strong love of wine, community, and Vancouver Island. With the help of a dedicated team of friends and family, and 25 acres of overgrown farmland, a vineyard was planted. Serendipity found the Windsors in 2014 when they stumbled upon an old German copper pot still stored in a barn on a Gulf Island, awaiting a new home. In no time, "Brunhilde," as they dubbed her, was brought back to DEVINE. Within a year, she had beautifully distilled her first DEVINE spirit: a strawberry eau de vie. DEVINE showcases locally sourced ingredients with its offering of certified craft whisky, gin, rum, eau de vie, vermouth, and wines—all made using traditional small-batch techniques.

The dedication to terroir is evident across all of DEVINE's spirits from the local honey for their Honey Shine to the unique blend of local, heritage grains in the Ancient Grains. The distilling team works hard to source and use ingredients as close to the farm on the Penisula as possible.

GOLDEN MANHATTAN

1 1/2 oz (45 mL) Ancient Grains
3/4 oz (22.5 mL) Moderna Vermouth
1/4 oz (7.5 mL) clove syrup
2 dashes of Angostura® Aromatic Bitters
2 dashes of Fee Brothers Black Walnut Bitters

Glass: Large Cocktail glass
Method: Stir all ingredients with ice
and strain
Garnish: Orange twist

Created by Jayce Kadyschuk

ESQUIMALT
WINE COMPANY

**Esquimalt
Wine Company**
3–859 Devonshire Road
Esquimalt, B.C. V9A 4T5
esquimaltwine.ca
250-213-7517

Core Products
Barrel-aged
Rosso Vermouth
Dry Vermouth
Kina-Rouge
Rosso Vermouth

Rye Barrel Aged
Rosso Vermouth
Gin Barrel Aged
Rosso Vermouth

What started out in 2015 as small soda company (Rootside Soda, producing soda syrups made with fresh and whole ingredients) evolved into a boozier venture for Quinn Palmer and Michela Byl. Attending a vermouth-centric event in 2017 at Vancouver's Odd Society Spirits (the makers of BC's first Vermouth) distillery opened the floodgates to the magical, weird and awesome world of apéritif wines and vermouth. There was no turning back; they just had to start making vermouth themselves. The pair spent the next two and a half years deep-diving into botanical research, recipe development, and wine-making to make its Rosso Vermouth (launched July 2019), which was a resounding success with. the first two batches sold out within a day of release. Expect to see lots more weird, herbal, apéritif wines in the near future.

VERMOUTH & TONIC!

3 oz (90 mL) Dry Vermouth
3 oz (90 mL) sparkling water
¾ oz (22.5 mL) Rootside Classic Dry Tonic Mix

Glass: Stemless wine glass
Method:Build all ingredients over ice and gently stir
Garnish: Lemon twist

**Phillips Fermentorium
Distilling Co.**
2010 Government Street
Victoria, B.C. V8T 4P1
fermentorium.ca
250-380-1912

Core Products
Stump Gin
Discovery Dry
Citrus Gin

Seasonal Products
Small Talk Whisky

Conceived by the minds at Phillips Brewing & Malting Co., the Fermentorium is a distilling house that launched in 2014, where unrestrained creativity and a hand-crafted approach shape unique recipes of all kinds. It is a place where old-world craftsmanship meets modern techniques; spirits are artisanally distilled in tandem on a classic 1920s Scottish British copper still, affectionately christened "Old George," as well as a modern German-built still.

Their first spirit, Stump Gin was designed with the west coast in mind, grand fir tips harvested when perfectly ripe, bay leaves from an old tree by one of the brewers house and the classic brewery ingredient of cascade hops.

OLD FASHIONED SMALL TALK

2 oz (60 mL) Small Talk Whisky
1/2 oz (15 mL) simple syrup
3 dashes of house-made citrus bitters

Glass: Old fashioned
Method: Pour all ingredients into glass and stir with ice
Garnish: Two skewered cherries

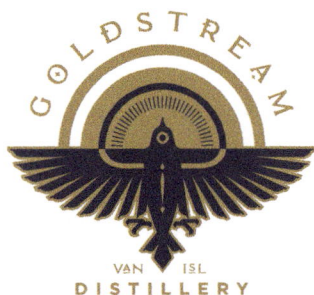

Goldstream Distillery
4A–4715 Trans-Canada Highway
Whippletree Junction, Duncan, B.C.
goldstreamdistillery.com
250-213-8476

Core Products
Goldstream Vodka
Goldstream Gin

Seasonal
Goldstream Whisky

Kathleen and Darcy Tringhams, along with longtime friend and partner, Colin Cumberbatch, moved the distillery from its original location in Duncan down to Whippletree Junction and have been operating there since mid-2019. As a relatively new distillery in BC, their long-term goal is to create spirits that reflect their little corner of the Island and expand beyond the Malahat across the province.

Along with its core products, such as vodka and gin, Goldstream has produced a three-year-old whisky distilled with Saskatchewan rye and finished in a unique barrel of toasted Brazilian Cherry Wood.

THE GOLDSTREAM

1 ½ oz (45 mL) Goldstream Vodka
½ oz (15 mL) Triple Sec
white cranberry juice

Glass: Highball
Method: Build all ingredients over ice and top with white cranberry juice
Garnish: Lime wedge and fresh mint

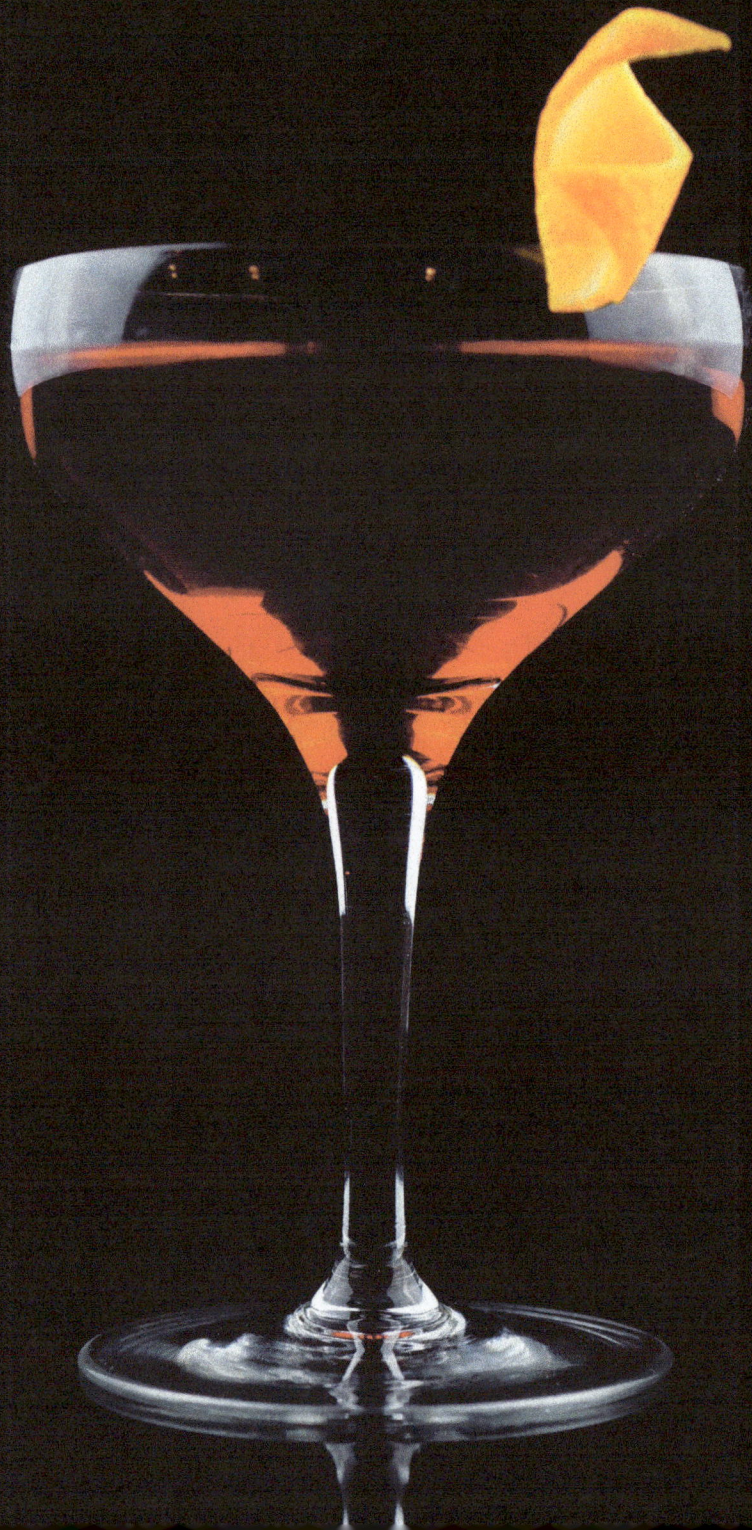

Core Products

Apple Dessert Cider	Cowichan Pear Brandy
Cowichan Cider Brandy	Cowichan Rhumb
Cowichan	Cowichan
Cherry Brandy	Spiced Rhumb
Cowichan	Cowichan Vodka
Cherry Liqueur	Cowichan XXO Brandy
Cowichan Copper Gin	Oaked Harvest Cider
Cowichan Gin	Whisky Jack's

Merridale Cidery & Distillery
1230 Merridale Road
Cobble Hill, B.C. V0R 1L0
merridale.ca
250-743-4293

In 2006, Merridale expanded its farm-based cidery into a distillery, and in 2013 it became B.C.'s first provincially certified craft distillery. Merridale proudly transforms B.C.-grown ingredients, both wild and grown at its Cobble Hill Farm, into delicious and distinctive spirits. Merridale distills in a 200-litre hand-hammered copper pot still, which provides the flexibility to make aromatic brandies, gins, and deliciously smooth vodka. All of Merridale's spirits are distilled at least twice, then aged for years in oak barrels their XXO brandy, cherry brandy and pear brandy are all aged for over a decade, stainless steel tanks, or glass containers until they reach their peak flavour.

COWICHAN STAR

1 oz (30 mL) Cowichan Cider Brandy
1 oz (30 mL) Esquimalt Wine Co. Rosso
1 barspoon Apple Dessert Cider
1 barspoon Merridale Hop Honey
simple syrup
2 dashes of Peychaud's Bitters
1 dash of Angostura® Aromatic Bitters

Glass: Cocktail glass
Method: Stir all ingredients and strain
Garnish: None

Created by Josh Nelson

MISGUIDED SPIRITS DISTILLERY

Misguided Spirits Craft Distillery
18–1343 Alberni Highway
Parksville, B.C. V9P 2B9
misguidedspirits.ca
250-616-8386

Core Products
Brother XII Vodka
Spectral Gin

Darrell Bellaart founded Misguided Spirits in 2016. A former print journalist with an interest in distilling, Bellaart's distilling dreams were given a nudge by the 2016 closure of the *Nanaimo Daily News*. The Misguided name was playfully adopted in the fall of 2018 and provided some much-needed comic relief after it was discovered that a previously registered business name was, in fact, unavailable.

Misguided Spirits Craft Distillery betrays a seriousness towards the craft of distilling. Officially opened in January 2020 after an 18-month build-out, Misguided only uses the best B.C. distilling wheat and Island-malted barley to create Brother XII Vodka, painstakingly distilled so that the grain flavour carries through into every shot. Only the best cuts are used for a surprisingly smooth vodka with a taste like nothing else.

Located four kilometres east of Coombs on the Alberni Highway, Misguided Spirits invites vistors to linger in its minimalist tasting room, which emphasizes the company's smaller-is-better approach, right down to the size of batches.

BROTHER IN BOMBAY CAESAR

1 oz (30 mL) Brother XII Vodka
¾ oz (22.5 mL) Misguided Spirits Gin
2 dashes of Tabasco sauce
4 dashes of Worcestershire sauce
Sons of Vancouver Chili Vodka, to taste
4 pinches of celery salt
1/3 oz (10 mL) lime juice
Clamato®

Glass: Highball, rimmed with celery salt
Method: Build over ice and stir, then top with Clamato juice
Garnish: Three skewered queen olives and a lime wedge

Created by Darrell Bellaart

Moon Brewery & Distillery
350 Bay Street
Victoria, B.C. V8T 1P7
moonunderwater.ca
250-380-0706

Core Products
Citrus Gin
Espresso Vodka
Moon Shaft Liqueur
Naked Stroll in the
Forest Gin (collaboration with Sister Cider)
Orange Vodka
Pure Grain Vodka

Seasonal Products
Blueberry Liqueur
Blackberry Liqueur
Candy Cane Schnapps
Chocolate
Orange Vodka
Local Strawberry Gin
Red Shiso Spirit
Green Shiso Spirit
Sloe Gin
Spruce Tips Gin
Strawberry Liqueur

Moon Distilling Co. was founded in November 2017, shortly after the 5th Anniversary of the Moon Under Water brewery. Moon Distilling Co. was started by brewmaster Clay Potter, his mother, Anne Farmer-Ash, and his stepfather, Steve Ash. Potter and Ash started home-distilling in Ash's garage in 2010, following Potter's return from Scotland, where he received his master's degree in brewing and distilling sciences and his IBD diploma in distilling. Since then, the pair have been creating a wide variety of vodkas, gins, and liqueurs, using as many locally sourced ingredients as possible like the recently released Naked Stroll Gin in collaboration with Sister Cider featuring a base of Island Grown Barley and BC Wheat then triple distilled with a wide range of botanicals from wild foraged BC Juniper, Grand Fir Tips, Spruce Tips, Lime Zest, Rose Petals, Lavender Tea, Grains of Paradise, Pink Peppercorns, Lime Leaves, Bay Leaves, and Cardamom Leaves, all while aging barrels of Scottish- and Irish-style whiskies and B.C. rye.

BLOOD MOON

2 oz (60 mL) Red Shiso Vodka
1 oz (30 mL) house-made berry coulis
½ oz (15 mL) lime juice
soda water

Glass: Cocktail glass
Method: Shake all ingredients with ice and double stain. Top with soda water
Garnish: Lime wheel

Created by Chamron Erikson

Pacific Rim Distilling
2–317 Forbes Road
Ucluelet, B.C. V0R 3A0
pacificrimdistilling.ca
250-726-2075

Core Products
Humpback Vodka
Lighthouse Gin

Pacific Rim Distilling is a small-batch craft distillery operating out of Ucluelet. tarted by Luke Erridge, a fourth-generation distiller, the distillery was built entirely by hand by Erridge and his 73-year-old grandfather. Erridge has refined old family recipes, which date back to the pre-Prohibition era, for the modern palette. Every ingredient that goes into Pacific Rim's spirits is from British Columbia and all the spirits are fermented using a wild yeast culture from Barkley Sound. Pacific Rim Distilling is a true craft distillery that uses no automation in any of its processes. Erridge uses time-tested traditional family whisky techniques to make one-of-a-kind Barkley Sound-style spirits even down to harvesting yeast from the local forest and only using locally foraged ingredients from around the distillery.

HEARTWOOD

2 oz (60 mL) Lighthouse Gin
1 oz (30 mL) Esquimalt Wine Company
Rosso Vermouth
3 dashes of Bittered Sling Kensington Bitters

Glass: Small cocktail glass
Method: Stir all ingredients with ice
and strain
Garnish: Orange peel

**Salt Spring Shine
Craft Distillery**
194 Kitchen Road
Salt Spring Island, B.C. V8K 2B3
www.saltspringshine.com

Core Products
Apple Pie Moonshine
Hive Vodka
Honeycomb Moonshine
Sting Gin

Owners Rie and Mike Papp studied at Le Cordon Bleu Paris in London, England, and opened a bistro in Georgetown, Ontario. They left Ontario and lived in Japan for two years before returning to Canada. Upon their return, they purchased vacant land on Salt Spring Island, which they cleared to build a house, and a studio for the distillery. Salt Spring Shine has truly been built by hand; Mike built entire studio from the foundation to the kitchen cabinets and used plenty of raw-edge maple that originally came from the property itself. Mike worked at Gary Oak Winery and learned everything from growing to fermenting. The distillery now focuses on fermentation of local honey, all our spirits are crafted and bottled by hand on the distillery farm.

SALT SPRING 75

1 ½ oz (45 mL) Sting Gin
1 oz (30 mL) lemon juice
1 oz (30 mL) Frostbite Elderflower Cordial
Prosecco

Glass: Flute
Method: Shake all ingredients (except Prosecco) with ice, strain, and top with Prosecco
Garnish: Lemon twist

Created by Rie Papp

Shelter Point Distillery
4650 Regent Road
Campbell River, B.C. V9H 1E3
www.shelterpoint.ca
778-420-2200

Core Products
Canada One Vodka
Shelter Point 150
Shelter Point Artisanal
Single Malt Whisky
Shelter Point Double
Barrel #5
Shelter Point Hand
Foraged Botanical Gin
Shelter Point
Montfort 151
Shelter Point Ripple
Rock Whisky

Shelter Point Single
Cask Edition 5
Shelter Point
Sunshine Liqueur
Shelter Point
The Collective
Shelter Point
The Forbidden

Seasonal Products
Shelter Point
Smoke Point

Established in 2011, Shelter Point Distillery is located on 380 acres in Oyster River, about halfway up the eastern coast of Vancouver Island. Farmed for generations, Shelter Point remains one of the last seaside farms on Vancouver Island. It's here where the distillery is naturally blessed with the key ingredients for exceptional, handcrafted artisanal spirits: fertile fields to grow barley, a large underground aquifer to provide naturally filtered water, and crisp sea air—compliments of the Salish Sea. Add in Shelter Point's skilled craftspeople, traditional Scottish distilling methods, and state-of-art facility, and the result is a world-class distillery on Canada's West Coast . In recent years, Shelter Point has become famous internationally for crafting world class single malts and whiskies that have garnished the attention from critics and journalists everywhere, with their goals firmly set on making their distillery and Campbell River internationally famous.

SHELTER PUNCH

1 ½ oz (45 mL) Shelter Point Artisanal Single Malt Whisky
¾ oz (22.5 mL) Shelter Point Sunshine Liqueur
½ oz (15 mL) Giffard strawberry syrup
¾ oz (22.5 mL) lime juice
1 oz (30 mL) pineapple juice
soda water

Glass: Mason jar
Method: Shake all ingredients (except soda) with ice and strain over fresh ice. Top with soda water
Garnish: Charred pineapple wedge, cinnamon, and lime wheel

Sheringham Distillery
252–6731 West Coast Road
Sooke, B.C. V9Z 0S9
sheringhamdistillery.com
778-425-2019

Core Products
Akvavit
Coffee Liqueur
Kazuki Gin
Seaside Gin
Vodka

Seasonal Products
Barrel-aged Akvavit
Rhubarb Gin
Whisky (multiple varieties)

Sheringham Distillery was founded in 2015 by husband and wife, Jason and Alayne MacIsaac. Jason had spent the previous 15 years as a globetrotting professional and private chef. He brings an incredible palate of flavours and taste profiles to the spirits. Alayne brings a decade plus of sales and marketing experience from the high-end apparel business.

Sheringham's spirits have won a multitude of international awards, the most prestigious being "World's Best Contemporary Gin" at the 2019 World Gin Awards, held in London, England. Sheringham benefits from Jason's incredible ability to balance flavours, and the unique power of one secret ingredient from the Pacific Ocean: *Alaria marginata*, more commonly known as winged kelp seaweed.

Originally in the small township of Shirley, the distillery made the move to Sooke Proper in 2018 to a bigger facility and dedicated tasting room. This has allowed them to expand their offerings and innovate further with their spirits.

PINK FLAMINGO

1 oz (30 mL) Sheringham Seaside Gin
2 oz (60 mL) watermelon juice
1 sprig fresh mint
1/3 oz (10 mL) Lychee Liqueur
2 oz (60 mL) Cucumber Soda

Glass: Highball or collins
Method: Build in glass, add ice, and stir
Garnish: Mint sprig

Created by Ryan Malcolm

Stillhead Distillery
105–5301 Chaster Road
Duncan, B.C. V9L 0G4
stillhead.ca
250-748-6874

Core Products
London Dry Gin
Vodka
Wild Blackberry Gin
Wild Blackberry Vodka

Seasonal Products
Apple Brandy
Barrel-aged Gin

Stillhead Distillery is a family-owned and operated craft distillery located in the heart of the Cowichan Valley. With a passion for whisky and other spirits, Brennan Colebank left the tech sector and pursued his dream of opening a distillery. Colebank opened Stillhead in 2017 with the help of his wife, Erika, and his parents, Ron and Christal. With love, passion, and the help of a loyal customer following, the Colebanks have been able to put away unique whiskies for aging, while releasing some uncommon spirits, like Wild Blackberry Gin. Using a custom 500-litre Arnold Holstein hybrid column pot still, Colebank and his team handcraft small batches to ensure they are producing to the highest quality product possible. From the fermentation process through to bottling, each step is done by hand, on premise, and from scratch. Their whiskies were released in late 2020, starting with a unique barrel-finished rye and a Hungarian Oaked Single Malt.

GERANIOL GIN COSMO

1 ¾ oz (52.5 mL) Stillhead London Dry Gin
¼ oz (7.5 mL) Arbutus Limoncello
½ oz (15 mL) cranberry cordial
½ oz (15 mL) lemon juice
1 dash of Ms Better's Bitters lack pepper cardamom bitters
3 snap peas

Glass: Large cocktail glass
Method: Muddle snap peas, add all ingredients, shake with ice, and double strain
Garnish: None

Created by Mitch Poirier

Core Products
Beach Fire
Espresso Vodka
Jalapeño Vodka
Old Growth Cedar Gin
Psychedelic
Jellyfish Absinthe
Rose Hibiscus Gin

Small Batch Vodka
West Coast Gin
Seasonal Products
Lavender Mint Gin
Limoncello

Tofino Distillery
681 Industrial Way, Units G & H
Tofino, B.C. V0R 2Z0
tofinocraftdistillery.com
250-725-2182

Founded by local volunteer firefighters John Gilmour, Adam Warry, and Neil Campbell, Tofino Distillery officially opened in June 2018 and is proud to be growing through 2020 with multiple expansions in both production and distribution. Their mission continues to be focused on sustainability, the environment, and the community—locally in Alberni-Clayoquot, across Vancouver Island, and all throughout the beautiful province of B.C. All the distillery's practices have been organic since Day One, and the distillery received its organic certification in 2019. The barrel program in Tofino is constantly growing, with a much anticipated a future in the whisky industry. In the meantime, on their next trip to Tofino, spirit lovers can taste the truly unique and authentic Psychedelic Jellyfish Absinthe, a spirit rich in history and lore that is a must for any bar, both at home and in restaurants.

BEE'S KNEES IN THE ROSES

2 oz (60 mL) Tofino Distillery Rose Hibiscus Gin
1 oz (30 mL) lemon juice
¾ oz (22.5 mL) honey syrup
soda water

Glass: Highball
Method: Shake all ingredients (except soda) with ice, strain over fresh ice, and top with soda water
Garnish: Lemon slice and rose petals

VICTORIA •
DISTILLERS

Victoria Distillers
9891 Seaport Place
Sidney, B.C. V8L 4X3
victoriadistillers.com/
250- 544-8217

Core Products	Oaken Gin
Brandy	Sidney Spiced
Chocolate Liqueur	Victoria Gin
Empress 1908	Vodka
Left Coast Hemp Vodka	

Victoria Distillers opened its doors in 2016 after 10 years of producing some of B.C.'s finest handmade small-batch spirits under the name Victoria Spirits. Founded by Master Distiller Peter Hunt, Victoria Distillers is located in the small, beautiful, seaside town of Sidney. The distillery creates a regional focal point at a site that is unmatched anywhere in the province, in terms of both its natural setting and environmental sustainability.

The distillery's most famed spirit, Empress 1908 gin, is a collaboration between Victoria Distillers and British Columbia's legendary Empress Hotel. Handcrafted in small-batch copper-pot stills using eight botanicals, Empress 1908 is the perfect combination of exquisite taste, delicate aroma, soft texture, and a remarkable indigo colour, which provides the perfect base for a new aesthetic of cocktail creation and enjoyment.

EMPRESS AND TONIC

2 oz (60 mL) Empress 1908
3 oz (90 mL) Fever-Tree Elderflower Tonic

Glass: Wine glass
Method: Build ingredients over ice and gently stir
Garnish: Grapefruit slice

Wayward Distillery
2931 Moray Avenue
Courtenay, B.C. V9N 7S7
waywarddistillery.com
250- 871-0424

WAYWARD
D I S T I L L E R Y

FUNDAMENTALLY AGAINST THE GRAIN

o o o

Core Products	Seasonal Products
Char #3	Garsten's Plunder
Cocktail Elixir	Garlic Vodka
Depth Charge	Ghost Pepper Vodka
Drunken Hive Rum	Raspberry Ginger Vodka
Krupnik	Char #3
Unruly Gin	Cocktail ElixirA variety
Unruly Vodka	of barrel-aged spirits

Wayward Distillery in the Comox Valley is Canada's first distillery to produce spirits using 100 per cent B.C. honey. In 2014, Dave Brimacombe and his team opened Wayward, a certified B.C. craft distillery celebrates spirits culture by making Unruly Gin, Unruly Vodka, Krupnik, Drunken Hive Rum, and Depth Charge. Each and every one of Wayward's spirits is precisely designed to be sipped on its own and enjoyed in the tastiest of cocktails. Honey is a delightful and sustainable resource, and Wayward is proud to support B.C. agriculture. Wayward loves how delicious its honey-based spirits are, and feels good about aligning its business with people who are also deliberate in their consumption choices, contributing to a healthy and diverse ecosystem.

In the last few years, Wayward has built two demonstration hives, lovingly cared for by local beekeeper Rachel, so that we can help educate our guests and community about the value and need for healthy honey-bee populations. We work with an apiary in the Peace Region of BC who care deeply about the health and long term sustainability of pollination, bees, and BC grown agricultural produce. When not out pollinating, the bees rest on clover fields, resulting in honey production that is supplied to Wayward Distillery.

When we first started working together, the apiary had 300 hives - we've grown, so they've been able to grow up to 1,700 hives. That means more food, grown by BC farmers, is being pollinated by BC bees. Wayward is a net positive food producer.

DRUNKEN HIVE RUM SOUR

2 oz (60 mL) Drunken Hive Rum
1 oz (30 mL) lime juice
1 oz (30 mL) honey syrup
1 dropper Ms. Better's Vegan Foamer
3 drops Bittered Sling Western Haskap bitters

Glass: Large cocktail glass
Method: Dry shake all ingredients, then wet shake, and double strain
Garnish: Luxardo Maraschino Cherry

VANCOUVER AND LOWER MAINLAND

The Lower Mainland of the province encompasses a huge expanse environments that vary in density and even climates. The abundance of diverse and unique distilleries here take full advantage of this amazing region in which they live and work.

From the farmlands of the Fraser Valley to the foraging-rich forests in the Coastal Mountains, these distilleries have an abundance of ingredients to incorporate into their products. Some use the out-of-the box primary ingredients such as corn, potatoes, and even blueberries to make their distillates, while. others delve into local botanicals collected by local foragers for gins and unique liqueurs.

101 Brewery & Distillery
1009 Gibsons Way,
Gibsons, B.C. V0N 1V7
the101.ca
778-462-2011

Core Products

The 101 Vodka	The 101 Gin
The 101 Aged Gin	Ericaceae
	Blueberry Liqueur

Since its inception in 2017, the 101 Brewhouse & Distillery has been bringing people together on the Sunshine Coast. Owners David Longman and Chris and Kelly Greenfield wanted to provide a venue for impassioned individuals to create, experiment, and share. The 101 is all about quality products and the belief that they can be fashioned in your own backyard. Originally an automotive mechanic shop, the 101 work-shop of today honours its blue collar roots with an entirely new form of craftsmanship. The first establishment in the area to merge craft beer, small-batch spirits, and locally inspired dishes, 101 has now a well-rounded community hub conveniently located on the Sunshine Coast Highway. Through urban-inspired flavours and a West Coast feel, the 101 strives to create an authentic experience representing the region and the style that epitomizes our vision.

PURPLE SUNSET

1 oz (30 mL) The 101 Gin
1 oz (30 mL) The 101 Ericaceae
Blueberry Liqueur
1 oz (30 mL) Blue Curacao
1 oz (30 mL) lemon juice
1 oz (30 mL) lime juice
soda water

Glass: Large cocktail glass
Method: Shake all ingredients (except soda water) with ice, double strain, and top with soda water
Garnish: Four blueberries on skewer and lemon wheel

Created by Mark Reed

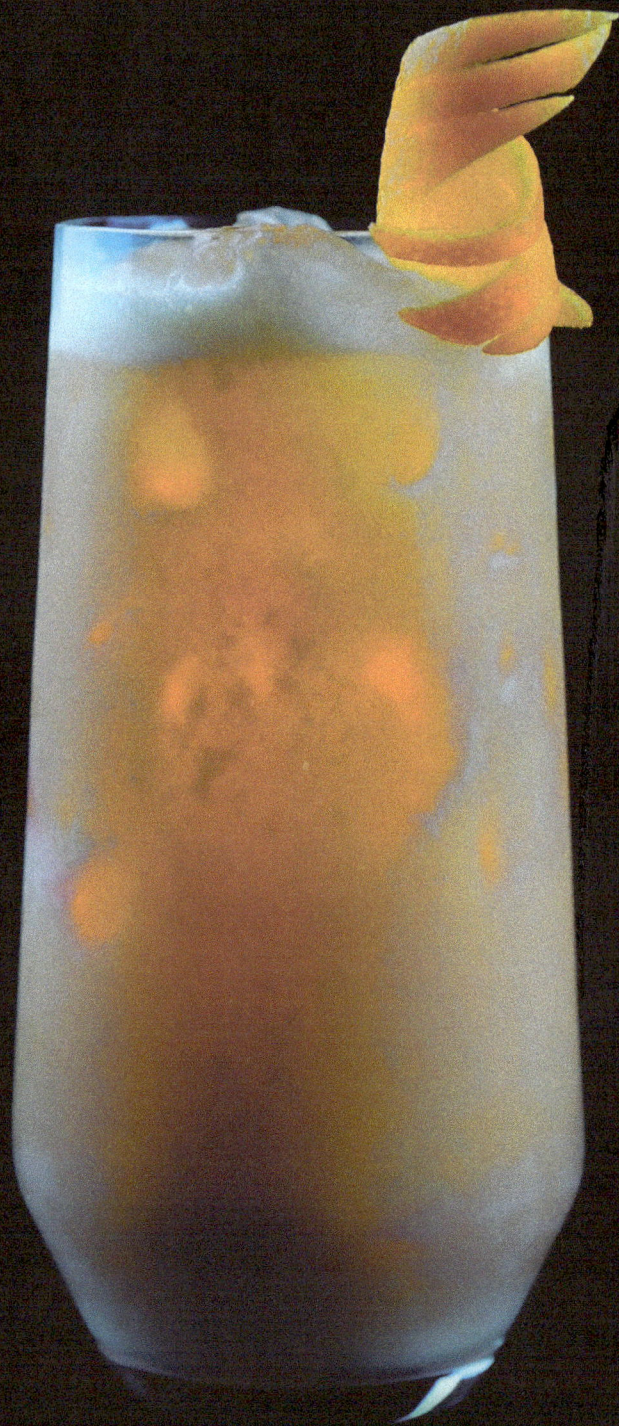

Bruinwood Estate Distillery
2040 Porter Road
Roberts Creek, B.C. V0N 2W5
bruinwood.com
604-886-1371

Founded in 2018, the idyllic Bruinwood Estate Distillery is located on a quaint farm in the heart of Roberts Creek. Operated by husband and wife team, Jeff Barringer and Danise Lofstrom, both former television producers, Bruinwood is quickly becoming known for its comfortable, yet elegant environment, original art, quirky high-quality, flavourful spirits, and exceptional customer service.

Core Products
Advocaat
Akvavit
Aquasen Vodka
Bruinwood Gin
Plains Vodka

Seasonal Products
Blackberry Vodka
Blackcurrant Gin
Chocolate Vodka
Crème de Cassis
Earl Grey Gin
Espresso Vodka

Figures Liqueur
K'Neko Honey Liqueur
Mandarin
Orange Vodka
Mocha Cream Liqueur
Nucino
Pechuga Espiritu
Pumpkin Spice Liqueur
Rhubarb Gin
Spirited Horchata
Quince Gin
Vanilla Vodka
Yorkshire Gin

ORANGESICLE

2 oz (60 mL) Advocaat
1 oz (30 mL) Aquasen Vodka
Jones orange soda

Glass: Highball
Method: Build ingredients over ice, top with Jones orange soda.
Garnish: Orange twist

Created by Danise Lofstrom

Central City Brewers and Distiller
11411 Bridgeview Drive
Surrey, B.C. V3R 2N1
centralcitybrewing.com
604-588-2337

Core Products

Lohin McKinnon 150th Anniversary Lightly Peated Malt Rye Whisky
Lohin McKinnon Chocolate Malt Whisky
Lohin McKinnon Lightly Peated Whisky
Lohin McKinnon Niagara Wine Barrel Aged Whisky
Lohin McKinnon Peated Whisky
Lohin McKinnon Single Malt Whisky
Queensborough Dry Gin

Queensborough Pink Raspberry Gin
Queensborough Omakase Japanese Gin
Queensborough Wine Barrel Aged Gin
Sparrow Rum

Seasonal Products

Lohin McKinnon VQA Black Sage Single Malt Whisky
Lohin McKinnon Tequila Barrel Finished Whisky
Lohin McKinnon Thomas Haas Cocoa Aged Whisky

Central City opened its distillery in 2013, commissioning a new production facility and expanding its brewing operation out of its modest brewpub in central Surrey. After three years of experimentation and development, it released Queensborough Gin, a uniquely West Coast gin crafted with hand-selected botanicals including juniper from the Canadian Rockies and spruce tips from Vancouver Island. Queensborough Gin was honoured with a Double Gold medal in 2017 from both the San Diego and San Francisco international spirits competitions.

One year after the launch of Queensborough Gin, Central City released Lohin McKinnon Single Malt Whisky (named for brewmaster Gary Lohin and head distiller Stuart McKinnon) to great acclaim. When it first appeared, Lohin McKinnon was one of the few Canadian single-malt whiskies produced in the Scottish tradition and created from a wash made from 100 per cent barley malt. Lohin McKinnon has since won numerous awards. The brand has also spawned multiple innovative and unique expressions, including a tequila barrel-finished whisky, a single malt made using 20 per cent chocolate malt in the wash, and a peated variant made from 100 per cent Scottish peated malt.

CHOCOLATE OLD FASHIONED

2 oz (60 mL) Lohin McKinnion Chocolate Malt Whisky
2 dashes Aromatic Bitters by Christos
1 barspoon demerara sugar

Glass: Old fashioned or rocks
Method: Stir all ingredients with ice and strain over fresh ice
Garnish: Flamed orange peel

COPPER SPIRIT DISTILLERY

Copper Spirit Distillery
441 Bowen Island Trunk Road
Bowen Island, B.C. V0N 1G0
copperspirit.ca
778-895-9622

Core Products
Presence Vodka
Verity Rye Spirit
Harmony Dry Gin

In 2014, Miguel and Candice Kabantsov conceptualized a distillery and lounge on Bowen Island—they wanted to provide welcoming space for their community to connect and experience clean craft spirits. Five years later, Copper Spirit Distillery opened its doors on July 1, 2019 welcoming both locals and visitors from around the world. Fuelled by a passion for creating the healthiest cocktails possible, Copper Spirit Distillery uses sustainable practises and exclusively organic grain, yeast, and cocktail ingredients.

PINK PEPPER GRAPEFRUIT SOUR

1 ½ oz (45 mL) Verity Rye Spirit
3 oz (90 mL) pink grapefruit juice
¼ oz (7.5 mL) local honey
1 egg white
6 dashes of Sado Maso Orangegasm Bitters
1 heavy pinch crushed pink peppercorns
1 heavy pinch of pink Himalayan salt

Glass: Large cocktail glass
Method: Dry shake all ingredients, then wet shake with ice, and double strain
Garnish: Pinch of crushed pink peppercorns

Created by Candice Kabantsov

DEEP COVE

BREWERS AND DISTILLERS

**Deep Cove Brewers
and Distillers**
170–2270 Dollarton Highway
North Vancouver, B.C. V7H 2M9
deepcovecraft.com
604-770-1136

Core Products
Mediterranean Gin
Barrel Aged Akvavit
Vodka

Seasonal Products
Canadian Rye Whisky
Frontier Whisky

Since its inception in 2013, Deep Cove Brewers and Distillers' focus has been to create fine spirits using B.C. ingredients. Direct from farm to glass, Deep Cove maintains close relationships with each of their local suppliers to ensure that every batch is created with the best ingredients they can find. From its humble beginnings as a small distillery and tasting room, Deep Cove has experienced open arms from spirit lovers, allowing them to not only produce flagship spirits, but also an expanding array of limited offerings for their customers. Their distilling equipment now runs around the clock to ensure no customer runs dry. The lounge and kitchen have been created to compliment the array of spirits and beers available and allows customers to experience their products as they have been intended.

CEDAR SOUR

2 oz (60 mL) Cedar-infused Vodka
1 oz (30 mL) lemon juice
1 oz (30 mL) apple simple syrup
1 egg white
3 dashes Bittermens Elemakule Tiki® Bitters

Glass: Cocktail glass
Method: Dry shake all ingredients, then wet shake with ice, and double strain
Garnish: Lemon peel and three drops of bitters

GILLESPIE'S
Fine Spirits Ltd

Gillespie's Fine Spirits
8–38918 Progress Way
Squamish, B.C. V8B 0K7
gillespiesfinespirits.com
604-390-1122

Core Products
Gastown Shine
Wheat Vodka
Lemoncello
Raspberry Gin
Sin Gin

Seasonal
Aphro
V-Twin
Café Crema

Gillespie's Fine Spirits was founded by Kelly Ann Woods and John McLellan in 2013. In their years of operations they have been trailblazers in the craft distilling scene and in building a craft beverage culture in Squamish. Their cocktail bar, The Squamish G Spot, and their spirits have won multiple awards, including the 2019 RBC Canadian Woman of Influence Award (Micro-Business Category).

ELDERFLOWER SOUR

2 oz (60 mL) Sin Gin
½ oz (15 mL) Boozewitch Elderflower Elixir
1 barspoon Boozewitch Peach Lavender Shrub
1 egg white (or aquafaba)
¾ oz (22.5 mL) lemon juice

Glass: Large cocktail glass
Method: Dry shake and then wet shake all ingredients with ice and double strain
Garnish: None

THE LIBERTY DISTILLERY

ESTᴰ 2010

HAND CRAFTED. TRADITIONAL SPIRITS.

The Liberty Distillery
Units 1 and 2 - 1494 Old
Bridge Street
Granville Island, Vancouver
B.C. V6H 3S6
thelibertydistillery.com
604-558-1998

Core Products
Endeavour Gin
Endeavour Old Tom
Endeavour Pink Gin
Railspur No. 1—White
Railspur No. 2—
Wildflower Honey
Railspur No. 3—Switch
Trust Whisky—Single Grain
Trust Whisky—
Canadian Rye
Trust Whisky—Southern
Truth Vodka
Truth Oat Vodka—
Distiller's Reserve

Seasonal Products
Endeavour Origins
Trust Whisky—Single
Cask Madeira
Trust Whisky—Single
Cask Burgundy

Established in 2010 on Vancouver's historic Granville Island, The Liberty Distillery is a true craft distillery. Selecting only the best B.C. organic grains, it carefully ferments, then triple distills in traditional hand-crafted copper pot stills to produce ultra-premium quality spirits with true character and distinction.

The Liberty Distillery strives to be traditional, classic, quirky, knowledgeable, and fun. Its enthusiastic team invites customers to step back in time at its 110-year-old saloon bar to taste classic old-fashioned cocktails, or to enjoy one of the distillery's signature creations. The uniquely crafted drinks range from the familiar to the astounding, but always show the beauty of its artisanal spirits.

THE TOM CAT

1 ½ oz (45 mL) Endeavour Old Tom Gin
¾ oz (22.5 mL) lemon juice
¾ oz (22.5 mL) Tuscany Pear Rooibos Tea Syrup
¾ oz (22.5 mL) Triple Sec
3 dashes peach bitters

Glass: Highball or collins
Method: Shake all ingredients with ice and strain over fresh ice
Garnish: Rosemary sprig and lemon twist

Created by Dominic O'Driscoll

Long Table Distillery
1451 Hornby Street
Vancouver, B.C. V6Z 1W8
longtabledistillery.com
604-266-0177

Core Products	Seasonal
Barrel Aged Akvavit	Absinthe
Bourbon Barrelled Gin	Amaro No. 1 Linnaeus
Cucumber Gin	Curacao
Langbord Akvavit	Marc du Soleil
London Dry Gin	
Texada Vodka	
Tradizionale Limoncello	

As ginsmiths and makers of premium spirits, the team at Long Table Distillery are inspired daily by the biodiversity of the untamed West Coast wilderness of British Columbia, from rugged coastlines and pristine waterways to alpine meadows and unique botanicals. Since becoming Vancouver's first micro-distillery back in 2013, Long Table has been passionately devoted to the fine art of copper pot distilling small-batch spirits, using noteworthy botanical blends that let their spirits speak for themselves. Long Table want is a place where kindred spirits meet to share in the love of the craft.

THE JOYCE

1 1/2 oz (45 mL) Long Table London Dry Gin
1 oz (30 mL) lemon juice
3/4 oz (22.5 mL) Ms. Better's Rhubarb Syrup
1 dash Ms. Better's Green Strawberry Mah Kwan Bitters

Glass: Large coupe
Method: Shake and double strain
Garnish: Dehydrated grapefruit crescent

Created by Tarquin Melnyk

Mad Laboratory Distilling
618 East Kent Avenue South
Vancouver, B.C. V5X 4V6
madlabdistilling.com
604-301-4855

Core Products
Blueberry Kombucha Cordial
Cranberry-Orange Kombucha Cordial
Mad Dog
Mad Lab Gin6

Mad Lab Vodka
ULKERaki
Viking Vodka

Seasonal Products
Black Cherry-Vanilla Kombucha Cordial

Founded by Scott Thompson in March 2015, Mad Laboratory was built with blood, sweat, tears, and almost no budget. Thompson had been a hobby distiller and liquor industry professional for 15 years before he decided to take the leap and build his own distillery. Confident about making fine spirits, almost all equipment was built from scratch, repurposed, or scrounged, and made into the setup that Mad Laboratory needed. If it wasn't absolutely necessary, especially in the early days, then it had to wait. Things have been a bit easier since Ahmet Ulker joined as a partner. Ulker is a fan of raki, Turkey's signature drink, hence the addition of Mad Laboratory's ULKERaki.

All current products come from a single-malt two-row barley mash, and are run through a custom-built stainless steel, direct-fire pot still, which makes for a rich and flavourful spirit with beautiful complexity and softness. This recipe and technique earned Mad Laboratory two gold medals in the 2019 Canadian Artisan Spirit Competition with, hopefully, more accolades to come. Mad Laboratory recently started its barrel program, which uses of ex-bourbon quarter casks from Oola Distilling in Seattle. Its anticipates that its first batch of whisky will reach maturity in November 2021.

PHILADELPHIA COLLINS

2 oz (60 mL) Mad Lab Gin6
3/4 oz (22.5 mL) lemon juice
3/4 oz (22.5 mL) simple syrup
1 oz (30 mL) Cranberry-Orange Kombucha Cordial
soda

Glass: Highball
Method: Shake first three ingredients with ice, strain over fresh ice, top with soda, and float cordial
Garnish: None

MAINLAND WHISKY

mellow & sweet

handmade in BC

Mainland Whisky
107–3425 189 Street
Surrey, B.C. V3S 0L5
mainlandwhisky.com
778-995-1841

Core Products

Cinnamon Whisky	Time Machine
Cherry Whisky Cordial	Whisky Triple Sec
Corn Whisky	Wildrose
	Whisky Liqueur

Steve Watts, the owner and distiller of Mainland Whisky in South Surrey, uses organic B.C. corn and malted barley to produce a mellow and sweet whisky reminiscent of his days in south Texas. All manufacturing is done on site, from mashing, fermentation, distillation, and bottling/barreling. Influenced by American whiskey recipes, Mainland makes small-batch corn whisky. Mainland Whisky's products are made in a hybrid reflux still with organic B.C. ingredients—no additives and non-chill filtered.

MAINLAND BREAKFAST

1 oz (30 mL) Mainland Corn Whisky
4 oz (120 mL) Earl Grey tea (chilled)
1 tsp. The Preservatory blueberry bourbon jam
1/2 oz (15 mL) lemon juice

Glass: Old fashioned
Method: Stir lemon juice and jam together, add other ingredients, and dry shake. Strain over fresh ice.
Garnish: Tea biscuit on the side

MONTIS
▲ DISTILLING ▲

Montis Distilling
1062 Millar Creek Road
Whistler, B.C. V8E 0S8
www.montisdistilling.com
778-996-7368

Core Products
North Vodka
Alpenglow Gin
Alpine Gin

Seasonal Products
Winter Spirit

Montis Distilling is a craft distillery owned by husband and wife team, Kwang and Bryanna Chen, in beautiful Whistler the very first distillery in the region. Since opening their doors in June 2019, the couple have focused on creating bold, distinctive spirits reminiscent of the wild, natural beauty of their environment. Launching a primary product line that includes North Vodka, a distinctively smooth sipping spirit, and Alpine Gin, made in the traditional London Dry style, with a cedar botanical twist, Kwang focuses on distilling complex and polished spirits that will elevate any cocktail experience. From grain to bottle, Montis Distilling runs its operation in the Function Junction neighborhood of Whistler, where locals gather for craft beer, notable eateries, and now, distinguished craft spirits.

BRÛLÉE COCKTAIL

2 oz (60 mL) Montis Vodka, infused with camomile
¾ oz (22.5 mL) lemon juice
1 ½ tbsp. cinnamon
1 ½ tbsp. Sunco Sultana raisins
1 ½ tbsp. nutmeg
¾ oz (22.5 mL) fine black pepper cordial
1 dash Dillon's Ginger Bitters
1 egg white

Glass: Large cocktail glass
Method: Shake all ingredients with ice and double strain
Garnish: Brown sugar, torched

Created by Damon Hanly &
Audrey Chamiot-Clerc

New Wave Distilling
3387 Tolmie Road
Abbotsford, B.C. V3G 2T9
newwavedistilling.com
604-864-1033

Core Products

Absinthe Minded	Disillusion Gin
Alpen Glow	Illusion Spirit
Bride's Tears	Lunar Gin
Cascade Gin	Rexford Rum
Cliffhanger	Riptide
Dawn Patrol	Summit Fever
	Valley Nectar

New Wave Distilling a family owned and operated distillery, located in East Abbotsford on the same property as its winery, Ripples Estate Winery. They use locally foraged and sourced ingredients from the Fraser Valley and surrounding areas, to create honest spirits with minimal environmental impact. New Wave's product line is inspired by the Fraser Valley and the surrounding mountains, rivers, and forests. Its spirits are made from 100 per cent organic blueberries, grown and picked on the family's blueberry farm along with local honey being used to produce their "rum style" spirit. The blueberries are then made into wine which they then distill to create their base spirit, which is then infused with flavours. New Wave's master distiller, Kelsey Mosterman, gleans her inspiration from the the diverse region around the distillery with farms, mountains and forests all influencing andinfusing her adventurous spirit into New Wave's products.

BLUEBERRY BASIL GIMLET

1 1/2 oz (45 mL) Disillusion Gin
1/4 cup of blueberries
4 fresh basil leaves
1/4 oz (7.5 mL) honey syrup
1/4 oz (7.5 mL) lime juice

Glass: Cocktail glass
Method: Muddle blueberries in shaker, slap basil leaves, add to shaker with the rest of the ingredients. Shake with ice and double strain
Garnish: Lime wedge and basil leaf

Created by Kelsey Mosterman

Odd Society Spirits
1725 Powell Street
Vancouver, B.C. V5L 1H6
oddsocietyspirits.com
604-559-6745

Core Products
Aged East Van Vodka
Bittersweet Vermouth
Commodore Canadian
Single Malt
Crème de Cassis
East Van Vodka
Oaken Wallflower Gin

Maple Canadian Whisky
Mia Amata Amaro
Mongrel
Prospector Rye Whisky
Wallflower Gin

Seasonal
Salal Gin
Elderflower

Founded by Gordon Glanz and Miriam Karp in 2013, Odd Society Spirits is a small-batch B.C. craft-certified distillery located in the heart of East Vancouver. Dedicated to combining old-world distilling traditions with new-world ingredients and ingenuity, Odd Society Spirits has created a family of spirits that entice and intrigue. Its award-winning lineup of spirits includes vodka, gin, amaro, vermouth, three distinct whiskies, and unique European-style liqueurs that celebrate locally grown ingredients.

THE SEER

1 2/3 oz (70 mL) Prospector Rye Whisky, infused with lapsang souchong tea
1 oz (30 mL) Aged Bittersweet Vermouth
1/2 oz (15 mL) House Chamomile-Honey Liqueur
3 drops saline solution

Glass: Chilled teacup
Method: Stir with ice and strain
Garnish: Zest lemon peel over the drink and discard

One Foot Crow
1050 Venture Way
Gibsons, B.C. V0N 1V7
onefootcrow.com
604-220-0550

Core Products
Cranberry Vodka
Gunpowder Gin
Handcrafted Vodka
La Vonne's
Lavender Gin

Mineral Infused
Gunpowder Gin
Mineral Infused Vodka
Rose Gin
A variety of bitters

One Foot Crow was established in 2017, in Gibsons on the beautiful Sunshine Coast. As a family owned business, One Foot Crow strives to bring art to the distiller's craft. They handcraft their spirits in small batches using 100 per cent B.C. grain and the pure waters of the Gibsons aquifer. One Foot Crow's signature gin and vodka are uniquely black, due to the infusion of 77 earth minerals. The distillery's interesting name comes from a one-footed crow that lived in the family's backyard. Friendly and curious, the crow was a great friend.

LAVENDER BEE'S KNEES

2 oz (60 mL) La Vonne's Lavender Gin
1 oz (30 mL) simple syrup
1 oz (30 mL) lemon juice

Glass: Large cocktail glass
Method: Shake all ingredients with ice and double strain
Garnish: Sprig of lavender

Pemberton Distillery
1954 Venture Place
Pemberton, B.C. V0N 2L0
www.pembertondistillery.ca
604-894-0222

FINE ORGANIC SPIRITS
PEMBERTON, BRITISH COLUMBIA
CANADA

Core Products
Aged Apple Brandy
Coffee Liqueur
Kartoffelschnaps
Organic Hemp Vodka
Pemberton Valley
Organic Single Malt
Schramm Organic Gin

Schramm Organic
Potato Vodka
The Devil's Club
Organic Absinthe

Seasonal Products
Blueberry Liqueur
Ginger Liqueur
Nocino Liqueur
Raspberry Liqueur

Established in 2008, Pemberton Distillery is one of B.C.'s original craft distilleries and the province's first certified organic distillery. Its mission is to express the character of the Pemberton Valley in the highest quality organic spirits. Pemberton Distillery makes it spirits in small batches, following the best of both modern and traditional methods implemented by Tyler Schramm, founder and master distiller.

THE HIGH MULE

2 oz (60 mL) Pemberton Distillery Organic Hemp Vodka
5 oz (150 mL) Fever Tree Ginger Beer
1 lime wedge

Glass: Highball or collins
Method: Build ingredients over ice and squeeze in lime
Garnish: Lime wedge

Created by Tyler Schramm

RESURRECTION

Resurrection Spirits
1672 Franklin Street
Vancouver, B.C. V5L 1P4
www.resurrectionspirits.ca
604-253-0059

Core Products
BC Dry Gin
Rye Whisky
White Rye

Seasonal
Oaken Gin
Pale Rye
Rosé Gin

Resurrection Spirits was founded in 2017 in the heart of East Vancouver. Owners Brian Grant, Adrian Picard, and Eudora Cheng operate the distillery and cocktail lounge. The focus of the distillery is rye and the different expressions into which Resurrection has transformed the grain. The cocktail lounge features a menu that changes five times per year to keep up with seasonal flavours. The Resurrection cocktail lounge regularly wows its customers with new flavours and offerings featuring its own unique spirits.

SCOFFLAW

1 1/2 oz (45 mL) Pale Rye
1 oz (30 mL) Dry Vermouth
3/4 oz (22.5 mL) pomegranate syrup
3/4 oz (22.5 mL) lemon juice
3 dashes Angostura® Aromatic Bitters

Glass: Cocktail glass
Method: Shake all ingredients with ice and double strain
Garnish: Dehydrated lemon wheel

Created by Brian Grant

Roots and Wings Distillery
7897 240 Street
Langley City, B.C. V1M 3P9
rootsandwingsdistillery.ca
604-371-2268

Core Products	Renegade
5th Element Absinthe	Sidekick
Double Vice Coffee	Vital Vodka
Encore Gin	
Jackknife Gin	**Seasonal**
Johnny Handsome	Hops and Honey
Old Fashioned Spirit	Cranberry Orange
Peachy Keen Vodka	Garlic Dill
Rebel	Dill Pickled Vodka

Roots and Wings Distillery founded in 2015 opened the doors in 2017 on a 30 acre farm in the heart of North Langley. Inspired by the land; the Distillers and Owners Rob Rindt and Rebekah Crowley, plant and harvest potatoes and corn to distill into unique and delicious spirits.

Not only growing the majority of the raw material to produce the base spirits but they also proof the spirits with the natural spring water from the farm which makes truly unique products to the region.

The tasting room, cocktail lounge, and farm-gate store is open year round with varying hours, and the option to host private events.

ONE DAY IN PARADISE

1 1/2 oz (45 mL) Cranberry Honey Orange infused Vital Vodka
3/4 oz (22.5 mL) Rootside Classic Tonic
1/4 oz (7.5 mL) Cara Cara balsamic vinegar
Dash orange bitters

Glass: Old fashioned
Method: Build over ice and stir
Garnish: Dehydrated orange wheel and frozen cranberries

Created by Rebekah Crowley

Salish Sea Spirits
7074 Westminster Street
Powell River, B.C. V8A 1C5
www.salishseaspirits.ca

Core Products
Vodka
Gin

Salish Sea Spirits was founded by Judi Tyabji, after years of planning and thinking. Jack Barr, operator of the Beach Gardens Resort & Marina, wanted a coastal craft distillery on site, and a partnership began.

Tyabji's father joined the B.C. wine industry in 1973; since then, she has worked in every aspect of agriculture. Tyabji's family operates a small heritage farm on the coast, which grows apples and blackberries. Her partner, Gordon Wilson, is a master of juicing the family's fruits, which made distilling a natural evolution. Wilson's son, Mathew, brings his experience in wine industry sales, shares a passion for craft distilling, and is in charge of business development. Partner, Sean Melrose of Rhiza Capital, provides sage business oversight, and Fenella Fownes of Optimist Design brought Tyabji's "mermaid and anchor" vision to life.

Tyabji found Lora Goodwin of Kootenay Country, and a collaboration was born to create the first production of Salish Sea Spirits out of B.C. honey in October 2019. In the fall of 2020, all production will be based at the Beach Gardens, with Seasonal Blackberry Vodka and Apple Gin on offer. In the winter of 2020, Salish Sea will cask their first whisky, which will be aged for three years, for tasting at Christmas 2023.

SIREN'S SONG

1 oz (30 mL) Salish Sea Vodka
¾ oz (22.5 mL) Blue curacao
¼ oz (7.5 mL) organic lemon juice
cranberry juice

Glass: Poco Glass
Method: Shake all ingredients (except cranberry juice) with ice, strain, and top with cranberry juice
Garnish: Lime wheel

SONS OF VANCOUVER

REALLY REALLY SMALL BATCH DISTILLERY LTD.

Sons of Vancouver
1431 Crown Street
North Vancouver, B.C. V7J 1G4
sonsofvancouver.ca
778-340-5388

Core Products
April Fool
Chili Vodka
Coffee Liqueur Sucks
Craft Blue Curacao
Craft Coconut Liqueur

No. 82 Amaretto
Vodka Vodka Vodka

Seasonal Products
Barrel Aged No.
82 Amaretto

Sons of Vancouver is a really, really small-batch distillery on Vancouver's North Shore. It was born out of a young, foolhardy desire to follow passions and contribute to a growing community of independent distillers. James Lester and Richard Klaus are the guys behind the curtain, who have created this selection of dynamic B.C. spirits using all the local ingredients have to offer from grains to honey and so much more.

Sons of Vancouver release real products on April Fool's Day that most companies just make a faux, fun product. These releases have included blue curacao, coconut rum and coconut creamer. This April Fool's reality is something that has become a yearly release

AMARETTO SOUR

1 ½ oz (45 mL) Sons of Vancouver No. 82 Amaretto (Peated Barrel Aged if you can)
½ oz (15 mL) Laird of Fintry Cask Strength Whisky
½ oz (15 mL) simple syrup
¾ oz (22.5 mL) lemon juice
2 dashes of Ms. Better's Bitters Foamer

Glass: Old fashioned
Method: Shake all ingredients with ice and double strain
Garnish: Cherry

The Spirit of Tea
106–3011 Underhill Avenue
Burnaby, B.C. V5A 3C2
www.thespiritoftea.ca

Core Products
Earl Grey Black Tea-
infused Gin
Vanilla Rooibos Liqueur

Founded in 2017 by Del Tamborini, in collaboration with Anderson Distilleries, The Spirit of Tea by Tayera Beverages Ltd., offers a line of premium tea-infused spirits. Blending the simple, artful elegance of tea with the vibrancy of British Columbia's spirits, The Spirit of Tea products are a fresh, sophisticated, and fun take on infused alcoholic beverages. The distillery has launched two products: a London Dry-style gin infused with an Earl Grey black tea, and a liqueur infused with a rooibos tea blend with Madagascan vanilla.

DUTCH BATH

2 oz (60 mL) The Spirit of Tea Earl Grey Black Tea-infused Gin
1 oz (30 mL) lime juice
3/4 oz (22.5 mL) cucumber syrup
4 dashes Peychaud's Bitters
2 sprigs dill

Glass: Old fashioned
Method: Combine all ingredients in shaker and give gentle muddle. Shake with ice and fine strain over fresh ice
Garnish: Dill sprig

Created by Guy Stowell

STEALTH
Craft Vodka

Stealth Distilleries
3–20 Orwell Street
North Vancouver, B.C. V7J 2G1
stealthvodka.com

Core Products
Stealth Corn Vodka
Stealth Wheat Vodka

Stealth Distilleries is a family owned and operated distillery in North Vancouver, B.C. Stealth Craft Vodka began in 2016 and was founded by John Pocekovic and operated by Randy Poulin, head Distiller. The pair pride themselves on creating excellent quality vodka … and *only* vodka, an exploration of how individual grains can taste in the final product; a unique take on the classic spirit. Stealth is proud to be from the North Shore and continues to build lasting relationships within its growing community.

BUSY BEE DRIVING A VESPA

1 ½ oz (45 mL) Stealth Corn Vodka
1 ½ oz (45 mL) Tugwell Aged Mead
2 dashes Bittered Sling Orange and Juniper Bitters

Glass: Small cocktail glass
Method: Stir all ingredients with ice and strain
Garnish: Ginger rosemary tincture

Created at The Mackenzie Room

The Woods Spirit Co.
1450 Rupert Street
North Vancouver, B.C. V7J 1E9
thewoodsspiritco.com
604-787-1735

Core Products
The Woods
Cascadian Gin
The Woods Limoncello
The Woods Amaro
Barrel Aged Amaro

Seasonal Products
Nocino

The Woods Spirit Co. combines scientific distilling methods, locally discovered ingredients, and an unbounded curiosity to create spirits ingrained in the outdoors. Born from the combined curiosity of a group of friends whose lives have been enchanted and shaped by the West Coast, The Woods Spirit Co. crafts genuine spirits that exist in an urban setting but reflect all the virtues of nature. Founded in 2016 by Fabio Martini, The Woods Spirit Co. strives to produce spirits that push boundaries, yet give a nod to the past.

THE CEVEDALE

1 1/2 oz (45 mL) The Woods Cascadian Gin
3/4 oz (22.5 mL) yuzu cordial
3/4 oz (22.5 mL) fermented yuzu juice

Glass: Cocktail glass
Method: Shake all ingredients with ice and double strain; mist with grapefruit extract
Garnish: Lemon twist

Created by Derek Boone

Yaletown Distilling Company
1132 Hamilton Street
Vancouver, B.C. V6B 2S2
yaletowndistillingco.com
604-669-2266

Core Products
Yaletown Vodka
Yaletown Gin
Yaletown
Mandarin Vodka

Seasonal Products
Yaletown Blue Gin

Yaletown Hop Gin and
Tequila Barrel Hop Gin
Yaletown Olde Oaked
Gin 3 Years French Oak
Yaletown Whisky 4
Years French Oak
Yaletown Whisky 5
Years French Oak

After almost 20 years of making fresh beer at the Yaletown Brewing Company, and pioneering the craft beer movement in Vancouver, it was an organic expansion for the Mark James Group to lead the way in artisan distilling. Launched on December 5, 2013, to mark Repeal Day—the anniversary of the end of Prohibition—the Yaletown Distilling Company is honouring the tradition of distilling by producing premium handcrafted spirits.

Head distiller Tariq Khan had been brewing for nearly 20 years in both Canada and the U.K. before shifting to spirits. The Distillery has the added advantage of being attached to an award winning brewery, working with Yaletown Brewing Brewers Josh Boyer and Riley Moynahan to begin the fermentation process and then passing it over to the distillery team.

TOKYO ROSE

1 ½ oz (45 mL) Yaletown Gin
1 oz (30 mL) sake
½ oz (15 mL) passionfruit puree
½ oz (15 mL) simple syrup
½ oz (15 mL) lemon juice
½ oz (15 mL) egg white

Glass: Large cocktail glass
Method: Dry shake, then wet shake all ingredients with ice, and double strain
Garnish: Rose petals

OKANAGAN AND INTERIOR

The Okanagan is the life blood of the province with ample fruit farms and orchards, sweeping acres of grains, and the world famous vineyards. This abundance of primary has lead to a truly unique dtyle of distillation in the valley. From the cold frigid northern end to the arid dessert in the south, the Okakanan Valley is home to some of the most eclectic distilleries in the province.

From niche eau de vie, heavy foraged ingredient forward and amazing lovally sourced fruit liqueurs, the Okanagan and interior is the epicentre of the exploration of terroir. Where distillers can take full advantage of literally what the next door neighbor is growing and turn it into something truly unique. This unique situation of both terroir driven and creative innovation has spawned a culture of completely Okanagan Valley specific products.

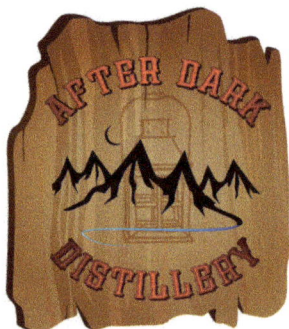

After Dark Distillery
1201 Shuswap Avenue
Sicamous, B.C. V0E 2V0
afterdarkdistillery.com
250- 836-5187

After Dark Distillery was founded by Dean and Louise Perry in 2016, after a long trek from Grand Prairie to Sicamous. Dean and Louise sold off their trucking company and made the move to build and open their dream: a craft distillery in B.C. After an eight-month building and licensing process, they started production in early 2017. After Dark produces a line of unique moonshines and whiskies with a small selection of gins and vodkas.

Core Products

After Dark Burner Vodka
Cinnamous Whisky
Copper Island Gin
Monashee Mountain Loud Mouth Soup
Monashee Mountain Moonshine—Apple Pie
Monashee Mountain Moonshine—Cherry
Monashee Mountain Moonshine—Espresso
Monashee Mountain Moonshine—Ginger & Honey
Monashee Mountain Moonshine—Hazelnut Coffee
Monashee Mountain Moonshine—Mountain Dew (original)
Monashee Mountain Moonshine—Peach
Monashee Mountain Moonshine—Root Beer
Monashee Mountain Vodka
Monashee Mountain Whiskey

Seasonal

Monashee Mountain Moonshine—Green Apple
Monashee Mountain Moonshine—Iced Tea
Monashee Mountain Moonshine—Lemonade
Monashee Mountain Moonshine—Mango & Peach
Monashee Mountain Moonshine—Maple

BCSPRESSO MARTINI

1 ½ oz (45 mL) Monashee Mountain Moonshine—Espresso
¾ oz (22.5 mL) Legend Distilling Blasted Brew
½ oz (15 mL) simple syrup
1 oz (30 mL) cold brew

Glass: Large cocktail glass
Method: Shake all ingredients with ice and double strain
Garnish: Three coffee beans

Alchemist Distiller
101–18006 Bentley Road
Summerland, B.C. V0H 1Z3
alchemistdistiller.ca
250-317-6454

Core Products
Libellule Gin
Nectar Apple Liqueur
Green Frog Absynthe
Mr. Fox Vodka

Originally from France, the Buttets—Sandrine, Simon, and little Zoe—started a micro-distillery in Summerland, B.C. in 2018. They designed their still in a very unique style, which allows them to extract the finest essences to produce very clean and flavourful spirits. All the products are made in small batches from local Okanagan apples and other natural ingredients.

GRANDAD'S AJ

1 ½ oz (45 mL) Nectar Apple Liqueur
¼ oz (7.5 mL) Lillet Blanc
¼ oz (7.5 mL) Green Chartreuse
2 dashes Angostura® Aromatic Bitters

Glass: Old fashioned
Method: Stir all ingredients with ice and strain over a large ice cube
Garnish: Lemon twist

BOHEMIAN
SPIRITS

Bohemian Spirits
215 Mark Street
Kimberley, B.C. V1A 2B2
bohemianspirits.com
1 800-919-2951

Core Products
Colossal Gin
Eclipse Coffee Liquor
Limited Gin
Vagabond Vodka

Seasonal Products
Forester Single Malt
Oak Aged Gin

Gin Sour
Harmony
Herbal Liqueur
Hearth Cherry Liqueur
Honeycomb
Cream Liqueur
Rose Rhubarb Ginger
Gin Liqueur

Bohemian Spirits was founded in 2014 by Wade Jarvis and Erryn Turcon in Kimberley, B.C. Jarvis and Turcon were committed to turning local grain into fine spirits. In 2019, the duo purchased a new location to introduce a proper cocktail lounge to Kimberley. As one of the only distilleries in the region, Wade and Erryn are constantly designing and creating new spirits for their loyal following throughout the province. Always be on the lookout for their latest offerings at the distillery and your local liquor store.

COLOSSAL GRAPEFRUIT COLLINS

2 oz (60 mL) Colossal Gin
1 oz (30 mL) lemon juice
1 1/2 oz (45 mL) ruby red grapefruit juice
1 1/2 oz (45 mL) simple syrup
soda water

Glass: Highball
Method: Build over ice, stir, and top with a splash of soda water
Garnish: Dehydrated grapefruit wheel

DUBH GLAS *Distillery* 🍁

Dubh Glas Distillery
8486 Gallagher Lake,
Frontage Road
Oliver, B.C. V0H 1T2
thedubhglasdistillery
778-439-3580

Core Products
Lockdown Single
Malt Whisky
Noteworthy Gin—
Navy Strength
Noteworthy Gin—
Barrel Rested Batch
Noteworthy Gin—New
Western Dry
Top Secret Liqueur
Smoke on the Water
Single Malt Whisky

Seasonal Products
Dubh Glas Single
Malt Whisky—Bottle
Strength Series
Dubh Glas Single
Malt—Cask
Strength Series
Dubh Glas Single
Malt Whisky—
Distillers Series
Virgin Spirits—Barley

Dubh Glas (dugh-*luhs*) in Gaelic means "from the dark water," and is reflective of the source water used in the making of their feature spirits; Dubh Glas sources pure "dark" water from a well on the property, which is fed by an underground aquifer. The source water from those dark depths has been filtered through the Okanagan Valley. The distillery's name is also reflective of Grant Stevely, the founder and artisan distiller, who has shared the name in his family for generations. Stevely began distilling operations in 2014 and officially opened the Dubh Glas Distillery doors in April 2015. It's not just about the whisky at the Dubh Glas Distillery—although it is their first priority. It's about a passion to create a distillery from the ground up that uses the finest raw products and materials available. From Canadian barley and select botanicals in its award- winning Noteworthy Gin, to the cooperage making the whisky barrels, every step of the process has been thoroughly researched before it is used in crafting their spirits.

Dubh Glas wants to showcase its products, however, it also wants to educate customers about the distilling process and highlight everything the world of whisky, gin, and spirits has to offer in the burgeoning craft distilling industry.

OLIVER'S TWIST

1 oz (30 mL) Noteworthy Gin—New Western Dry
½ oz (15 mL) Arbutus Distillery Elderflower Liqueur
½ oz (15 mL) lemon juice
½ oz (15 mL) chili-infused local honey
local lager

Glass: Highball or collins
Method: Shake first four ingredients with ice, strain over fresh ice, then top with lager
Garnish: Lemon zest and chili pepper

101

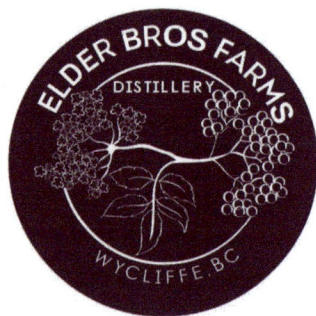

Elder Bros. Farms
3121 Mission Wycliffe Road
Cranbrook, B.C. V1C 7C8
elderbrosfarms.com
250-581-2300

Core Products
Elderflower Liqueur

Whack-a-Vole Apple
Strudel Schnapps
Whack-a-Vole
Elderberry Schnapps

Whack-a-Vole
Elderflower &
Honey Schnapps
Whack-a-Vole
Elderflower &
Cherry Schnapps
Whack-a-Vole Cherry &
Honey Schnapps

Elder Bros. Farms is located in beautiful and sunny Wycliffe, near Cranbrook. Here, the Lepsis family owns an 84-acre farm, which is home to more than 5,000 elderberry bushes that produce both fragrant elderflowers and healthy elderberries. Our base alcohol is fermented Creston cherries and apples with kosher schnapps yeast. Each bottle of raw schnapps is infused with a combination of cold-pressed elderberry juice, elderflower syrup, fresh cherry juice, fresh apple juice, cinnamon, and our local honey.

THE PINK LADY

1 ¼ oz (37.5 mL) Dubh Glas Noteworthy Gin
¾ oz (22.5 mL) Whack-a-Vole Cherry &
Honey Schnapps
1 oz (30 mL) lemon juice
1 oz (30 mL) egg white
½ oz (15 mL) Cocktail Merchant Hibiscus
Chai Syrup

Glass: Large cocktail glass
Method: Dry shake all ingredients then
wet shake all ingredients with ice and
double strain
Garnish: Three drops Peychaud's Bitters

Created by Harry Dosanj

FORBIDDEN
SPIRITS
DISTILLING CO.

**Forbidden Spirits
Distilling Co.**
4400 Wallace Hill Road
Kelowna, B.C. V1W 4C3
forbiddenspirits.ca
250-764-6011

Core Products   Forbidden Vodka
Adam's Apple Brandy   Rebel Vodka

Forbidden Spirits Distilling Co. the name comes from the apple being the prohibited fruit for Adam and Eve in the Garden of Eden., located on a picturesque property in southeast Kelowna, takes delight in capturing the purest essence of British Columbia's finest produce. Its small-batch process offers the time to carefully attend to each step from the orchard to the distillery to the cocktail in your hand. From it own apple orchard to its close relationship with local farmers, the distillery strives to use the finest local fermentables to craft an exquisite variety of seasonal spirits. Owner Blair Wilson and GM Marisa Vardabasso opened the Forbidden Spirits tasting room in May 2019, on 20 acres of natural beauty.

REBEL HONEY'D GIMLET

2 oz (60 mL) Rebel Vodka
¾ oz (22.5 mL) Okanagan Wildflower Honey Simple Syrup
¾ oz (22.5 mL) lime juice

Glass: Cocktail glass or coupe
Method: Shake all ingredients with ice and double strain
Garnish: Lime wheel

Created by Max Macdonald

Jones Distilling
616 Third Street West
Revelstoke, B.C. V0E 2S1
www.jonesdistilling.com
778-489-8018

Core Products
Gin No. 3—Strawberries & Cream
No. 4—Cranberry
Gin No. 5—Black Tea & Caramel
No. 6—Raspberry Leaf Tea
Gin No. 7—Rooibos Vanilla
No. 8—Berry Blend

Gin No. 9—Passionfruit & Orange
Gin No. 10—Rooibos, Cardamom & Orange
Mr. Jones Premium Vodka
Revelstoke Premium Gin No. 1

Seasonal Products
Go Big or Go Gnome
Sweet Spot

Jones Distilling is an internationally awarded and recognized craft distillery that creates small batches of premium vodka, gin, and alcoholic botanical cordials with B.C. ingredients. The distillery is named after owner Gareth Jones's father, a bit of a rogue who instilled a passion for the distillation process in Gareth, who grew up preparing botanicals for his father's creations.

In 2016, Jones Distilling found its home at the Mountain View School, a heritage building built in 1914 that has become a landmark on Third Street in downtown Revelstoke. The modern, open-concept tasting room is now set up in a former science classroom overlooking views of the Columbia River.

SPIKED CHAI LATTE

6 oz (180 mL) strong steeped chai tea
1 ½ oz (45 mL) Mr. Jones Premium Vodka
½ oz (15 mL) Galliano
½ oz (15 mL) half and half cream

Glass: Old fashioned
Method: Build ingredients over ice, with the cream last, stir with cinnamon stick
Garnish: Cinnamon stick

Legend Distilling
3005 Naramata Road
Naramata, B.C. V0H 1N1
legenddistilling.com
778-514-1010

Core Products

Black Moon Gin	Silver Moon Gin
Blasted Brew Spiked	Shadow in the
Coffee Liqueur	Lake Vodka
Doctor's Orders Gin	Slowpoke Sour
Harvest Moon Gin	Cherry Vodka
Honeymoon Gin	Slowpoke
Naramaro	Farmberry Vodka
Manitou Orange and	Slowpoke Strawberry &
Sumac Liqueur	Rhubarb Vodka
	Wyatt Whisky

Legend Distilling was founded in 2014 by Doug and Dawn Lennie. Their goal is to craft unique spirits from farm to glass in Naramata, which has been their home for the past 15 years. Legend Distilling use 100 per cent B.C. grains and local Naramata fruits and botanicals whenever they can to support other small businesses in their community and throughout the province. Legend's Restaurant and Lounge also operates, on-site with a similar mission of using local produce and suppliers.

NARAMATA NEGRONI

1 oz (30 mL) Silver Moon Gin
1 oz (30 mL) Manitou Orange and
Sumac Liqueur
1 oz (30 mL) Naramaro
Dash lemon bitters

Glass: Old fashioned
Method: Build over ice and stir
Garnish: Orange twist

Maple Leaf Spirits
948 Naramata Road
Penticton, B.C. V2A 8V1
mapleleafspirits.ca
250-493-0180

Core Products

Aged Italian Prune	Pear Liqueur
Apricot Liqueur	Pear Williams
Cherry Liqueur	Maple Liqueur
Canadian Kirsch	Italian Prune
Lady of the Cask	Skinny Gewürztraminer
Peach Liqueur	Skinny Pinot Noir
	Wild Apple

Pioneers in Craft Distilling in Penticton since 2005, Jorg and Anette Engel offer customers a unique experience on the Naramata Bench where most visitors are wine touring. They are proud to offer award-winning spirits, brandy, and liqueurs, all handcrafted from Okanagan-grown fruit, grapes, and wine, and distilled following European tradition. Customers can find classic Swiss-style Kirsch, Pear Williams, and several other fruit-based spirits. Maple Leaf Spirits is home of the famous wine brandy, the "Lady of the Cask," aged in oak barrels since 2010. Their fruit liqueurs celebrate sun-ripened Okanagan fruit, and are great as a lovely sweet treat on their own, or to enhance a dessert or cocktail. Also on offer in its tasting room on the Naramata Bench are a selection of single-varietal grappa, tresterbrand, and marc de vin.

CARROT CAKE

2 oz (60 mL) Lady of the Cask
1 ½ oz (45 mL) cardamom and carrot syrup
½ oz (15 mL) egg whites
pinch of cinnamon

Glass: Cocktail glass
Method: Dry shake, then wet shake ingredients with ice, and double strain
Garnish: Cardamom and carrot straw

Created by Margot Baloro

![Monashee Spirits logo]

Monashee Spirits
307 MacKenzie Avenue
Revelstoke, B.C. V0E 2S0
monasheespirits.com
250-814-7299

Core Products
Ethos Gin
Vulcan's Fire
Triticale Whisky
Bitter Hearts
Cocktail Bitters
Vodka

Seasonal Products
Absinthe
Bear Aware Fruit Brandy

Big Mountain Creamer
Blue Gin
Cherry Gin
Garlic Vodka
Huckleberry Gin
Plum Gin
Revelstoke
Coconut Rhum
Spruce Tip Gin
Strawberry Rhubarb Gin

Up amid the Monashee Mountains, in the town of Revelstoke, lies a small craft distillery and cocktail bar creating award-winning spirits from locally grown organic triticale grains. Monashee Spirits was founded in 2016, with a heavy foundation on local and sustainable practices, and a focus on collaboration among their community and friends. The distillery creates spirits and cocktails that represent the wild alpine surrounding this mountain town.

EGG NOG NOG FLIP

¾ oz (22.5 mL) Revelstoke Coconut Rhum
¼ oz (7.5 mL) Vodka, vanilla-bean infused
½ oz (15 mL) Cognac
½ oz (15 mL) French Brandy
¾ oz (22.5 mL) cane sugar syrup
1 oz (30 mL) cream
1 whole egg
2 dashes Bitter Hearts Aromatic Bitters

Glass: Small cocktail glass or Nick and Nora
Method: Combine and dry shake with shaker spring, add ice, and hard shake. Double strain into chilled glass
Garnish: Cinnamon lit on fire and grated nutmeg

Created by Josh McLafferty

Okanagan Spirits
5204 24 St, Vernon, BC V1T 8X2
267 Bernard Ave, Kelowna, BC V1Y 6N2
okanaganspirits.com
Vernon - 250- 549-3120
Kelowna - 778-484-5174

Core Products
Applejack IPA Whisky
Aquavitus
Barrel Aged Family
Reserve Gin
BC Rye Whisky
BC Hopped Whisky
BLK BRBN Cask
Strength Bourbon-Style
Corn Whisky
BRBN Bourbon-Style
Corn Whisky
Essentials BC Gin
Essentials BC Vodka
Evolve Gin
Family Reserve Gin
Family Reserve Vodka

Laird of Fintry Single
Malt Whisky

Laird of Fintry Single
Malt Whisky Rhum
Agricole Finish
Laird of Fintry Single
Cask Strength Whisky
Master Distiller's Series
Final Proof Whisky
Okanagan Shine Unaged
Corn Whisky
Taboo
Genuine Absinthe
A selection of fruit
brandies and liqueurs

Okanagan Spirits Craft Distillery is Western Canada's original craft distillery, dating back to 2004. The distillery sprung from the idea of using 100% locally grown fruits and grains to make premium, world-class spirits, just a tractor ride away from the orchards and fields where the base ingredients were grown. B.C.'s original harvest-to-flask distillery now offers a selection of more than 30 internationally-awarded spirits ranging from B.C.'s first single malt, rye and bourbon-style whiskies, to gins, vodkas, liqueurs, fruit brandies, aquavit, and Canada's Original Genuine Absinthe.

Okanagan Spirits is family-owned and operated. They work directly with their local farmers and foragers to truly capture the taste and aromas of the Okanagan Valley in every single bottle.

OK OLD FASHIONED

2 oz (60 mL) BRBN Bourbon-Style
Corn Whisky
1/4 oz (7.5 mL) Okanagan Spirits
Maraschino Liqueur
3 dashes Bittered Sling Denman Bitters

Glass: Old fashioned
Method: Stir all ingredients with ice and strain over fresh ice
Garnish: Orange twist and Okanagan Spirits Drunken Cherries

OLD ORDER
— DISTILLING CO —

Old Order Distilling Co.
270 Martin Street
Penticton, B.C. V2A 5K3
oldorderdistilling.ca
778-476-2210

Graham Martens, the owner and founder of Old Order Distilling Co., had a vision for creating a craft distillery in downtown Penticton, using traditional distilling methods to create unique premium spirits. Martens' family has been toiling with soils and crops for more than seven consecutive generations and have owned a small fruit orchard in Summerland since 1973. The family's venture back into distilling is a direct result of the provincial government opening the doors for the use of 100 percent B.C. grains and fruits from farms just like theirs.

CAFÉ GENIÉVRE

1 oz (30 mL) Legacy Gin
1 oz (30 mL) Patrón XO Cafe
2 oz (60 mL) espresso
1 barspoon ginger puree

Glass: Large cocktail glass
Method: Shake all ingredients with ice and double strain
Garnish: Three coffee beans

Taynton Bay Spirits
1701 6 Avenue
Invermere, B.C. V0A 1K4
tayntonbayspirits.com
778-526-5205

Core Products

Blueberry Rooibos Tea Infused Cocktail	Orange Turmeric Tea Infused Cocktail
Gin	Pickled Vodka
Ginger Matcha Tea Infused Cocktail	Raspberry Vodka
Hibiscus Bitters	Sinferno
Mint Lime Bitters	Strawberry Herbal Tea Infused Cocktail
	Sweet Orange Bitters
	Vodka

Taynton Bay Spirits, based in Invermere, B.C., was founded in 2017. Justin Atterbury and Steve Kofflerare passionate about producing clean label, easy to enjoy spirits. All of the distillery's spirits are made from locally sourced wheat, and then infused with natural ingredients, including looseleaf tea, fruit, spices, and honey. Taynton Bay's line of tea infusions are a hit, providing customers with 14 per cent ABV ready-to-serve cocktails.

BERRY FIZZ

2 oz (60 mL) Strawberry Herbal Tea
Infused Cocktail
1 oz (30 mL) Raspberry Vodka
3 oz (90 mL) Sprite

Glass: Highball
Method: Build over ice and stir
Garnish: Lemon wheel

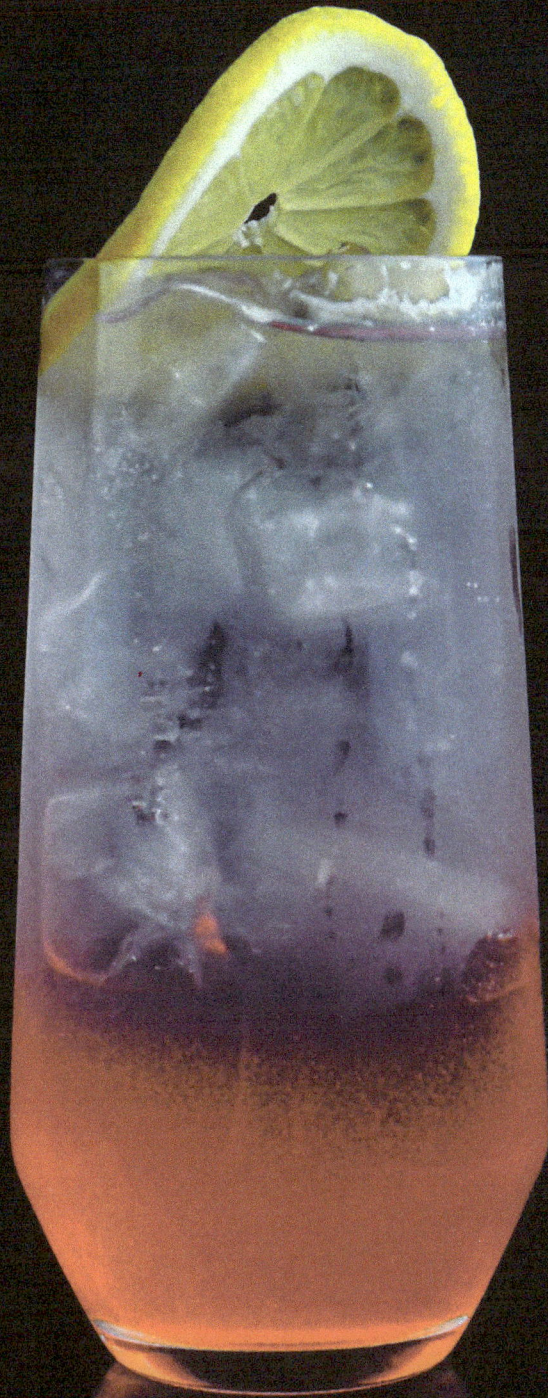

TRUE NORTH DISTILLERIES

True North Distilleries
1460 Central Avenue
Grand Forks, B.C. V0H 1H0
truenorthdistilleries.com
778-879-4420

Core Products
Area D 54-40
Black Dog After Dark
Scots Choice

Seasonal Products
Area D 668
Traditional Absinthe
Cherry Muscat

Green Hit
Djinneh Elderberry Gin
Dominion Rye
Hulda Rum
Hecate Spice Rum
Plum Brandy
Red Absinthe

True North Distilleries is the first female-owned and operated distillery in B.C. Founders Meghan and Heather Stewart make award-winning whiskies and liquors in Grand Forks. They focus on lightly-oaked spirits without sulphites and use and local and natural ingredients, which are processed by hand. True North supports local farmers and wildcrafters while producing their spirits for their loyal local clientele Some of their flagship products include: Highland Whiskey, Irish Style Whiskey, and Rye.

In 2020, True North won a National Gold Medal for its Cherry Muscat Liqueur and a National Silver Medal for its Area D 668 Absinthe at the Canadian Artisinal Spirit Awards. Over the last three years, True North also won three National Taste Medals for its whiskies. True North supports the Whiskey Wednesday Project and encourages everyone of drinking age to consider joining in and upping their game.

THUNDER AND LIGHTNING

1 ½ oz (45 mL) Hecate Spice Rum
Fever Tree Ginger Beer

Glass: Smoked pepper-rimmed large cocktail glass
Method: Rim glass, shake rum with ice for 10 seconds, strain, and top with ginger beer
Garnish: Lime twist

Created by Scot Stewart

WISEACRE
FARM DISTILLERY

Wiseacre Farms Distillery
4275 Goodison Road
Kelowna, B.C. V1W 4C6
wiseacrefarmdistillery.com
250-469-2203

Core Products
Lazy Ass Vodka
Single Malt Vodka
Gin No 13
Gin No 17

Seasonal Products
Limoncello
Lavender Gin

Lavender Liqueur
Rhubarb Gin Liqueur
Harvest Gin
Cranberry Liqueur
Cran-Orange
Gin Liqueur
Cran-Rosemary Liqueur
Peppermint Vodka

Nestled in six sweet acres of farm and forest, customers will find a tiny distillery in the woods. At Wiseacre Farm Distillery, there's an ample welcoming committee on arrival: one cow, two donkeys, one cat, two dogs, and a happy flock of pasture-raised laying hens. Customers can tour their collection of vintage farm equipment, wander the gardens, and then make their way to the quaint and rustic still house and tasting room.

After the unexpected passing of both her parents, Kristi and her husband, James, decided to leave their busy life in Metro Vancouver and return to the family farm that had been left to them. With their two young daughters along for the ride, they worked tirelessly to honour her parents' legacy, while forging a new path with the creation of the distillery. After nearly three years, Wiseacre finally opened its doors in December 2019.

They say, "it's the little things" that matter most. Wiseacre proves that to be true–by producing small-batch, quality spirits in their own cozy corner of East Kelowna. Each step in the production process is completed by hand, with the help of their passionate and nimble team. The philosophy and profile of their spirits is very much inspired by the farm they call home. With an ever-increasing amount of their ingredients growing just a stone's throw from the still house, they strive to keep their spirits as truly local as you can get.

THE LOVE LETTER

1 ¾ oz(52.5 mL) Wiseacre Lazy Ass Vodka
¼ oz (7.5 mL) Okanagan Spirits Maraschino Liqueur
1 barspoon Crème de Violette
½ oz (15 mL) rose petal syrup
¾ oz (22.5 mL) lemon juice
½ oz (15 mL) egg white

Glass: Large cocktail glass
Method: Shake all ingredients with ice and double strain
Garnish: Three drops of Bittered Sling Lem-Marrakech bitters and dried rose petals

Created by Bar None Okanagan

Wynndel Craft Distilleries
1331 Channel Road
Wynndel, B.C. V0B 2N1
wynndelcraftdistilleries.ca
250-866-5226

Core Products

Apple Liqueur	Forbidden Fruit
Apple Brandy	Brandy Liqueur
Apple Rum	Licorice Mint Liqueur
Apricot Brandy	Mixed Berry Liqueur
Apricot Liqueur	Old Tom Apple Gin
Apricot Schnapps	Old Tom Pumpkin
Butterfly Blue Gin	Pie Gin
Cape Grape Brandy	Peach Brandy
Cherry Brandy	Peach Liqueur
Cherry Liqueur	Saskatoon Brandy
Cherry Schnapps	Saskatoon Liqueur
Elderberry Liqueur	Saskatoon Schnapps
Floral Gin	Spicy Peach Vodka

Wynndel Craft Distilleries, located in the heart of the beautiful Creston Valley, is owned and operated by Pat and Jeanette Meerholz. The duo began production in 2017 and less than three years later they are producing over 20 varieties of hand-distilled spirits. Variety is the spice of life!

SASKATOON JULEP

1 oz (30 mL) Saskatoon Brandy
1 oz (30 mL) Saskatoon Schnapps
½ oz (15 mL) simple syrup
8 mint leaves

Glass: Julep mug
Method: Steep the mint in ingredients, add crushed ice and swizzle, then continue adding crushed ice until full
Garnish: Two big mint sprigs

ABOUT THE AUTHOR

What began as a youthful ambition to craft the perfect cocktail, has matured into a proficiency across every aspect of beverage service.

Twenty years after being named State Title winner by the Australian Bartenders Guild, Shawn Soole continues to view the service industry as a medium to deliver his unique style of exceptional customer experience.

From bar/restaurant concept creation, menu formulation, staff training and launch guidance, to branding, marketing and public relations strategies - Shawn's experience and advancement of the industry have been prolific.

Shawn has co-authored the books Cocktail Culture (2013) and Great Northern Cocktails (2019), and provides ongoing contributions to publications such as Liquor.com and EAT Magazine.

As a dedicated and vocal proponent of the industry, Shawn has presented keynote speeches (Lisbon Bar Show), increased public awareness for distillers in BC, Canada (BC Spirits) and continues to advocate his mission 'to make the industry better for everyone' (PostShift podcast.)

His input has been vital to the launch and/or ongoing success of numerous highly-acclaimed bar and beverage programs, such as Little Jumbo [2013], OLO [2015], Cafe Mexico [2016] and Pagliacci's [2018].

To accommodate his growing role as a consultant, Shawn founded Soole Hospitality Concepts (SHC) - a network of industry leaders with decades of multi-faceted experience. Together they provide innovative responses to all the needs of hospitality-oriented businesses.

His firm belief in the importance of consistent personal growth drove him to recently complete a diploma in Advanced Hospitality and Tourism Management (Camosun College), achieving a level of distinction that placed him on the Dean's List.

In 2019, Shawn traveled to Singapore to consult on the the conceptual development, systems implementation, and launch guidance for Miss Fitz and Roxy, two bars under the SOS Group banner. In 2020, he returned to the bar that started it all and took back over the multi award winning Clive's Classic Lounge.

INDEX BY DISTILLERY

INDEX BY COCKTAIL

CPSIA information can be obtained
at www.ICGtesting.com
Printed in the USA
LVHW071147170722
723693LV00009B/236